apparently

New Poems

GIRAMONDO POETS

joanne burns | apparently

First published 2019
from the Writing and Society Research Centre
at Western Sydney University
by the Giramondo Publishing Company
PO Box 752
Artarmon NSW 1570 Australia
www.giramondopublishing.com

Designed by Harry Williamson
Typeset by Andrew Davies
in 11/17 pt Adobe Garamond Pro

Printed and bound by Ligare Book Printers
Distributed in Australia by NewSouth Books

A catalogue record for this
book is available from the
National Library of Australia.

ISBN: 978-1-925336-99-3

other books by joanne burns

Snatch

Ratz

Alphabatics – children's stories

Adrenalin Flicknife

Radio City 2am – with Stefanie Bennett and Ruth K. Fordham

Correspondences – with Pamela Brown

ventriloquy

blowing bubbles in the seventh lane

on a clear day

penelope's knees

aerial photography

people like that

footnotes of a hammock

an illustrated history of dairies

amphora

brush

Contents

dial

planchettes

shucks

are you really a local
barramundi sing your tidal
runes like a wishbone lost in
a muddy gob, thalassic provenance
gone to pot where is the real
atlantis, no stevedore can vouch
for this, beef cake heritage or not;
you juggle the pregunta's cube like
a soda's augury but the bubbles
are flat the air tramps on, its
swag of lumbago daemonian
ether stuck in a rut –

amble

travel in the paganini
canoe and you'll never become
punctual   feed that sort of salad
to your favourite shark and it will
be pissing beetroot, and set off
an alarm   i finally located
your power of attorney doc [so
unreadable even bookworms had
only nibbled at the edges] in
the shredder handbook

your rare coin collection was
so rare i couldn't find it   if
you are intent on casual touring
don't get lost in the slush fund

i can hear your bones clicking
you are somewhere out there
in the etheric brambles but
your name is so outdated you
will need a new one – perhaps
several   you will be required to make
the purchase yourself

calypsonic

do you feel like a
tangible sailor your
hair chocka with
permanent waves, or
an insect posing as
a water nymph in
search of a new nickname –

nothing beats finding a location
with the best overall view the day
before you are born   a twelve
month commitment is sought
for this role   you must have a
capacity to yearn –

gummy

the première of alcopops
on the astroturf –

the odometer was no tamer
of jellyfish larceny tenderloin

moments in the harlequin surf
the revamped alumni executive

booked a course in psychoflorescence
in the yukon, etymology more

demure than balderdash

hallmark

mango scars on the
eiderdown   dead
ducks in the paisley
knee prints on the raisin
toast   wild oats absconding
down the gullet of the stainless
steel sink   a housemaid
hijacks a lear limousine
with a thimble of blood

                                        who
is drafting another crime fiction
so many fears after bedtime   cracked
wedgewood keens in the scullery

mission drift

the triathlon sedition needs
more than a hyphen   too much
sweat factor for something so abstract;
how could you make a decent
syllogism of it, too hard on the
footwear and the festivity gene –
for the prima facie vitamin load
tick borderline hallucinogenic it's
got altitude overload preferable
to file it under frenemy
of the state   so hopalong <u>now</u>
cursory glance

pennant

world politics gone queasy
the oligarch skates through
reclaimed savannah in his
alopecia jumpsuit, improvisation
shrewd as a hoodwinker monk –
time to hoist the vinyl archived
at the alpine sanitorium, all night
jam sessions over lake bassoon;
eventually treaties discreet as miniature
cutlets, abacus beads abandoned like
out of date beluga   a quartet of
cartographers flown in like sympathy
cards

planchette

the anarchy of sober
noodles   does the buck
stop here   crazy logic
of lava citadels   the swanky
ambiguity of matador pants
a breach in the futurosity of
time   blini addicts duck
and cover in their ancestral
glug boots down the blackholes
of juvenilia   cosy as irish moss

prospectical

tenderise that cold
shoulder with a comprehensive
study plan   the samurai option
the bean stalk epic   chocolate
block virtue   scholastic sunsets
on corrosive horizons   ruminate
for all your worth

wispering ballerinas frieze
along your cortex like graceful
vermin   time to fumigate the thesaurus
exhume the algebraic from the bottom
of the well –

tipsy

turning crustacean
not as easy as it sounds
that drooling hunger for
the international séancery
could hoist you out of that
haven of many high tides;
it's hard to shake claws
in a salt-reduced diplomacy
crunching the numbers ill
advised, descend to the lassitudes
of your genomic grottoes – and no
dreams of schmoozing st. augustine ~

apparently

detail

wedged in the doorway at an angle. a man leaning to the right. arms stretched up against the jambs. a very large man. not a giant but memorably tall. the height of a doorway. dressed in navy blue. boiler suit blue. large jaw. all this i noted briefly as i opened the door. he fell forwards onto the floor right away. i wasn't sure whether to call the ambulance or the police but i knew it was serious, though i wasn't nervous or particularly concerned. it seemed like something to remember when i woke up. i suppose it was what you might call a history lesson. i'm not sure whether i have failed or passed the subject. perhaps it's just another of those parentheses.

evaluation sheet

i didn't pop over to epidaurus to visit the theatre. see a spot of sophocles maybe. i dropped in to the sanctuary of asclepius purely to sleep. investigate my future. i entered the long hall of the enkoimeterion and lay down waiting for morpheus to download. in the dream i was offered a plate of what looked like boars' eyes smelling like leatherwood honey, and balls of cotton wool that cackled then buzzed like bees. i refused to make a choice between the two.

on the morning afterwards the wily priest who was contracted to help me understand my dream was too busy sipping freshly pressed virgin olive oil to engage with me. all he said was *work it out for yourself toots.*

that's the last time i do a self-improvement course for seniors in the ancient healing arts.

glyph

the slumbering eye is presented with a small silvery tablet displayed on its right side – a glimpse a tease. never to be explained entirely. tiny creatures moulded onto the metal. antique figures clinging to the edges. the tablet disappears before the mind has time to scrutinise what its sleeping eye has noted. here in retrospect these minute beings seem so intense, fragile, and tenacious. perhaps templates for a consideration of the underestimated soul.

hush

it was a shady house. perhaps californian bungalow in style. the air layered with fragments of quiet conversation in various corners, recessed spaces and rooms. the second time i visited i stayed for more than a glimpse through a slightly opened door leading off the hallway. i had decided to enter the room where brunch was to be provided on a quartet of small tables circling the figure on the bed. here a slender young man lay on his back, his long hair smooth and silky his countenance iconically posed. this must be jesus, the christ. but was he alive or dead. i considered the simple option – a small platter of pumperknickel, carraway rye bread, hummus and olives. then i needed a glass of water and left quite suddenly, preferring the archaeology of my own bed, its familiar comforts ~

para-graphic

a vaulted hall. an assembly, a reunion. visitation. figures stroll or gather round through the shadows of the columns. i passed you there, who once stirred my young heart, questioned the rhythms of my eager mind, my unconventional translations. how ordinary you looked in that obituary photograph, without those mysterious garments of disguise. the atmosphere grew redundant, unnecessary. i walked away further and further across the sequestered territory. how long it took, how far i travelled i do not know. but there it was, fresh and thrilling. this open land: green, benign and promising, its river vast as a horizon. such prolific recognition.

prima vera

the hostess was wearing a wimple. she offered me a flute of mead and a unicorn snack pack. detour travel was tattoed on her forearms. the hessian seat was starting to annoy my bikini.

whoever booked me on the flight forgot my luggage. i texted it to meet me at the whitsunday terminal. ‘how will i recognise you’ it replied. ‘by the ampersand in my hair’ i said.

prop

macbeth was coming up the stairs, for us to study. who were we? where was i?

it was a vast drawing room. groups of young unfamiliar women were arranged around various comfortable lounges. waiting.

was this some kind of finishing school or had i wandered there after watching a particularly intense episode of 'silent witness', where many young women had been murdered in a basement, each having had a finger cut off by the killer, a handsome bearded ex-policeman. clear plastic curtains streaked with blood hung in his laboratory.

i can't recall ever having seen 'macbeth' at the theatre though i may have; but i did see the polanski film version: that glint of duncan's crown spinning on the floor.

a copy of the play landed on the carpet next to the armchair i had appropriated, reminding me to stay in the present, tuned. ah, that's the one i last taught from: the hardback arden edition. durable and tough and still functioning after decades of mis-use.

and didn't we teenage virgins love to read the witches' lines in 1961.

although this burnished room was full it still seemed somehow empty. lady macbeth not here yet.

she will soon send a messenger – has been delayed. taking a long hot shower with norman bates, across the landing.

macbeth was coming up the stairs.

purchase

here is a long dark table with rounded bevilled corners. a finely crafted table. at first sight the wood seems smooth as velvet. one edge of the table is obscured by the absence of light where the rest of the room recedes.

—

you stand at the edge of the dream. close enough to touch the table but you don't. there is both an intimacy and a remoteness about its presence. you are aware that it is a new table. a gift perhaps. or a clever purchase. you had wanted to use the word 'mahogany' to refer to this table. you like its rhythm and length. but it lacked depth. the wood of the table has a burgundy tint. you know it belongs at present to a man who wants to harm someone through its agency. you don't know why or how. the atmosphere is unsettling but not quite sinister.

—

to refer to this moment as poe-like would be inaccurate. presumptuous. even kitsch. all you know is what you feel, so far. that everything will happen slowly. a glance. a short conversation. perhaps then a long lecture. the twist of a limb. the glare of an eye. the quiet pourings from a decanter attendant in the wings.

—

this tableau might well be a document of someone's trauma. the floorboards don't creak but the air shifts in almost imperceptible winnowings. the vertical turns concave. when 'trauma' from the greek arrived in the english lexicon around 1650 it referred to a physical wound. it has become so much more than its original denotation. a word of intradermal suffering, damage. there is something compelling about the word, so close in spelling and utterance to 'thauma': a wonder, a marvel. such propinquity. perhaps it is language itself that is the deceiver. the agent of unease.

—

the man moves closer. in his right hand he holds a bic pen. black. cristol m. a sharp line of light needles along its surface. this moment disappears.

—

two months of dreams later someone offers you a thick booklet of $100 notes in exchange for a small poem. but which what poem. the currency is too bright. the colour of cheap lime cordial. 'but i don't do sweet' you say. 'sorry'.

wheel : a documentary

solid. firm. grey coated. standing on pavement outside a bus depot in a quiet regent's street. a tall chiselled bus driver beside her. a yellow and green double decker parked at the kerb. it was enough. no need to speak or touch. the previous time i had encountered her i was wandering the front lawn of her long lived in cottage right near a bus terminus on the corner of the south head road, across from the old dairy and the sandstone cliffs sprayed with the moody lyrics of a hegemonic ocean. she had been agitated, fleeing across the moonlit sky, her white gown of ectoplasm thin and pale. i made it my business to smother my responses to this visitation beneath a thick wad of dreams. this inheritance that had overestimated its capacity.

dial

sting-along

there's no point to owning a country
if you can't look after your own hair
the tv burped   the weeks broke up like packets
of biscuits   we swept through them on the way
to the bus stop   holidays were full of conjunctions
forget the piles of prepositions   i ate crime novels
with a plate of siestas   my signature slid around
like a post-mexican wave; the insects were almost
worse than centrelink on every windowsill after
dark   the film about the poet with a neat little
notebook no crossings out was too cute for
words   i got sunburnt in the shade between
the mango and the bacon   the soles of my best
$200 sandals fell to pieces like archived echoes
during a free speech on heart attacks   send
a photo to our address in the bible belt advised
the manufacturer   the dog didn't eat the housework
it just got lost   time to vacate the vacation   i forgot
that my new super dental floss is not an astral chord

granary

there hungry children squat
in the concrete dust   stare
into numb verbs of a lens
caked in grey grains of attrition –
dry eyed gods offer zilch
contrition

here people brag about
buying a new car getting rid
of that old bomb have had it
since the sydney olympics   there
the car is the bomb and the bomb
is the car   plenty of roar then plenty
of scrap   in each place a metallic arena

celebrity chefs spray tables with palmfuls
of flour preparing fresh bakes for couchloads
of dilettante viewers   take care how you fold
the mixture   everyone eager to wolf it
down   this is the odour of history

chill

refrigerate the deal
pouting ain't pretty
when words lose
their mercantilist lisp
more wealth accumulation
in pursed jaw hibernation
imagine the dna bubbling
in that patriotic swamp while
the quack sleeps between the
lobster and the mousse   will there
be free gold curtains any time soon –

drain

the wind blew ~
a delinquent artery
hurtling along the parade
of the damned hopeful
slamming through sound
barriers with skateboard
precision   the leviathan
of apartment towers hits
another sinkhole who
pulled the plug in this
city of home improvement,
its duchies of power
drill rodeos   hold onto
your tickets and contracts if
that is your heart rate's
decision   but you won't
get your moolah back –
you're off the plan
though you've done all
the math on your i-phone
see those mass graves of
hard hats   rank drains
of delusion ~

nod

the breath of history
the murmur, roar
the silences   deep and
full and fresh   the dark
bush across the harbour
the rocks   the headland
the swimmers   seagulls on
the shore   a twilight moment
backdropped by all the smug
and lavish houses that recede
as you sit and sense the place
long before the tall ships came;
the notches in this blue ribbon
belt of harbour nod off like
discarded fancy dress

please be seated

sit down on the national values lounge
and stand up with vertigo   should
that be vice versa   the policy banquet
squeaks like a lazy susan   i can say this
without fear or flavour   here is a mind
make-up app from the duty-care party
the ballot paper tinged with blush   buffed
slogans, safe as tweezers

model citizen

is it a deal
always that juggle
with the bubble
the intimate triangle
of the talentoidal clock
brief bun burgers laced
with secret hooks ~ ~
hi carb and barb how
fries lie   a bikini backed
career on the sand; patriot
koalas hit the ground running
like scouts

press

a dataset glut risk
geographically concentrated
apartments   wobble like notional
agreements   heebie jeebies   heckle
and jeckle are coming to peck you out
in the flat pack airflows   executive
breakdowns in subtower carparks   status
details so quo   commemorative coins joyride
above karmic clouds   remuneration surrenders
to cardboard shoes   press the elevator
button   we're going down

appetite

did you notice the one
who pounds down the freeway
as if he's a castle –
bulldust scratches the mineral
sutra's throat   potluck or
potash lurching through back
alleys   a scrum of rodents
on the tenemental rooves;
buckets list like weary
crocs in old moët
billabongs   a music of
bankrupture flares across
dedicated screens   an appetite
for rage, or rave?

bushranger beardos versus
blazer gangs   it's a close
shave

visions splendid stink
dead fish in the think
tank
hear those schooners clink

pro-tractor

or *is there a better time to vote*

the market creeps
cat burglar or
backfence thug
dissension hovers like
three dollar shop drones
bulk billing lurches off
the backs of trucks
deceased estates
detention centres discard
geometry or was that
cartography   compassion disappeared
by a parliament of sinkholes   do you
know the difference between a LED light
leadlight and a donation led economy – compulsory
question 2 for the renewal of your ID cards

kale catches in the dentures like another
amateur interview issues surface and periscopes
whinge   organic vegetables squeak and shine so
real you'd think they were plastic   what are your favourite
rebates 1–5   psephology's a growth industry
like paleo churches   i'm allergic to candied dates

when is a mate not a mate –
when they are a mate   *correct*

cynicism is the new chewing gum
pink as difflam

innovate – a revamped resort
full of vacant suites

dispatch box

i.

you show us how you stir
a giant vat of chocolate paste
stirring like a kid, pouring in hundreds
of bright smarties or were they m&ms
hmmm..... these little buttons, studs
sink into the confected waves, the
sweet swirl of political can-do   no
job too simple no job too tough for
you on the ocean, or the factory floor

ii.

you announce the arrival of a hot new
product, tangerine [no not pea-green]
lifeboats to fill with ninety human ingredients
or more – is this a cartoon or a toyworld fest:
sealed unsinkable for export delivery across
the waves no customs duty forms
required   on arrival just get out
and walk –

iii.

along our sovereign coast, waterways, and harbour
shores sleek white watercraft gleam and purr with
plutocratic pride   wealth's privacy has been dispatched
offshore to safer havens; fortunes seek asylum at
a tap, a tweak, a fingertip: a flotilla of touch pads

aurora

the parsnip lagoon
makes it difficult
to breathe   no air
pockets in the apron
jutting northwards, best
to aim for the ocean
road regardless of a
cordillera of camp ovens
furphying the credentials
of the golden roast

are you aware of
the devictualisation
psalms   last words
last supper   there'll be
giant fronds of ghost kelp
cajoling through your aura
tonight –

compensation

excitement   a revised
flyover to choctop
boredom   so let's sip
prosecco like white
chiffon flutologists
how those 3d-eed
bubbles tickle your
fancy   i went to
the wrong movie but
had the right ticket
for an emergency tax
deduction   i'm sorry
i can't remember the
director's name was it
fellini, bergman, or taran-
tino   everyone seems to rush
out before the credits start
to roll – i'm indebited to
the reliability of an elevator
even if the traffic lights insist
on being stubborn   the spring
water is half the price across
the rheumatoidal road   they call
it tank stream spa   well did you
bring your pack of loyalty cards

the optional anchovy

held with casual yet careful
reverence   the fresh and warm
flat box is transported
through the streets with comestible
conviction; this quotidian purchase
secretes an aura and protection
that sacred scriptures might
invite   revelations intricate
and bright as mandalas, or a stained
glass fenêtre – pizza with pieta –
no burnt offerings from the makers'
divers ovens   that myth of loaves
and fishes might need a quick rewrite

when the hours turn cold the boxes
are discarded in the gutters or the bins
the only scriptural remnants on their
damp insides: a shadowy stale oratory
of diminished fat

breakfast at the end of a financial year

bodies become corpses at the whim
of a machine gun rising up from
carthaginian waves   no more suntans
or lotophagi breakfasts by the sea
houellebecq you warned us but who
is so cognisant when a holiday is
urgent like a first or last resort
v-a-c-a-t-i-o-n   wimbledon is
second best   squalks of cockatoo
hijack talk of those treasonable
tweets   tennis brats make threats
parents slurp back ego shakes
as children morph to instant geniuses
or genii on rapid break-the-fast tv
coffee brews avocado smash and
feta bites into the burnished toast
the acropolis in the distance stoic and
forlorn   syntagma spreads like vertigo-a-go
-go; here comes cautionary ritsos as he drags
his bags of stones, scratching like the claws
of tiny owls along the ground   will those
sydney lentil counters graduate to quinoa
numerology dukka delphics million dollar
bedsits or simply chocolate frogs   just
mind the gap between the trireme and the pier
dock   no ATMs ahoy   fate curves like a recycled
frisbee in search of destiny –

floral

red check tablecloths
at the sincere pizzeria
no camouflage for
the banana topping
[cabanossi or not]
the pink chemist so
pink nausea pills
overdose on themselves
half a dozen police guns
wobble like buttocks as
they escort extra large
coffees back to headquarters
hundreds of french fries scatter
across the road like abandoned
romance

keyboard

coin inacup here's a milkcrate
linguist instant noodle meeting potts
point poodle pique explosions along
the golden mile a battered telephone
dangles after a drug deal mangle in the
pissed off phase 000 to go a deficit of
glory how happy *is* that happy hour, naive
tequila squealer why not have a contemplative

spritzer at the photogenic
fountain, sacred as a spindly homer
in the setting sun pinochet-ed of late
by a ring of stark black bollards as snappy
tourists circulate, weekend urinals proliferate –
evangelists pluck out their whiffy
tunes

clutching clipboard quizzes girls in party
hats romp by making notes on cop
shops adult entertainments colourful identities
conserved on grubby pavement plaques   such
enthusiastic squizzers this surge to win a prize

ibis scratch their arcane dialects into the random
rubble   the duke of darlo-road's ghost, his face
still glowing like a roast, begins to rattle that
lavish chain of keys =

snob

don't think i'll hear
a fly buzz when i die
more likely a voice booming
instructions on where to queue
for the official passage   there being
a jam in the tunnel   some spirits
rushing to cross the river   others
determined to rush back to life in
time for the latest sports event or
extra season of celebrity chef –

i'd like to die a more *easeful*
death to the rhythm of a slow
light breath   like a final exercise
in pranayama   thinning down to
a miniature mmnn ~   lifting towards
a familiar vastness an expandable
yonder   the 'me' now a drift of
prodigal particles   not szymborska's
'to vanish like a spark' :
                    but a generous
                    sabbatical or silky gap year
                    before the next reassignment –

                      no dog or horse or rat perhaps
                      something more extra-terrestrial

balance sheet

not just a case of dizzy lizzy:
two weeks of vertigo   i'm gone gone
there's no hitchcocked glamour   this
is the season of struggling with even
quotidian grammar

cold and wet and sweaty as a curse
of medieval weather my head lurches
side to side to resuscitate an absent
spirit level

no smooth or smart enjambments
slanted rhymes, to claim emiliana
where that *plank in reason broke*
just a swarm of clammy grey caesuras

no confected charm of a sitting buddha
to distract me   i'm splayed upon
that raft of the medusa

swivel

the swivel chair. its screws are loose. it sits and stares. it roominates. who is the lodger of this room. packed to the ceiling with cupboards, tables, book shelves, cabinets, ziggurats of books and papers lurching across a cluttered carpet. a room spilling with ornaments, clothes, shoes, luggage, icons, jewellery, pictures, photos, medicine, documents and decorations, perfumed oils, paper clips, machines and manuscripts. an embarrassed emporium. a reckless junkyard. is this an autobiography. does this room own itself. the original owner shoved out the door. a refusal to change. its peeling ceiling, dusty carpet, creaking floorboards.

its plantation shutters with their redolence. its views. this is a room with a view. a view to the sky. a sky blue view through another clear, uncovered top floor window in the distance. reaching up like a magritte theatre.

is this a room of its own. more and more books. draped with african middle eastern vietnamese indian scottish scarves and shawls. dental bills secured with seashells. more shoes spilling over yet more books. goya borges ashbery szymborska the bucolic poems of vita sackville-west. a postcard of caravaggio's st. francis leaning on a roll of packing tape. old superannuation statements sharing space with newspaper obituaries. ayn rand's journals adjoining dry mouth gel and allergy pills. gertrude stein meets enid blyton meets dickinson.

the room is resilient, prescient. long suffering. it loves its patterned plaster ceiling. it writes its own poems. prints its own books. this room can sing its version of allegri's miserere. spem in alium. sings bob dylan. can insist like a wide mouthed greek tragedy. it defies the propaganda of the clutterphobes and busters. the book burners. it owns three second hand copies of fahrenheit 451. they are intact.

this room broods like an eternal hen. i pick and swivel in its glorious mess.

bound

a small book with a varnished
wood cover bound with leather
flowers from the holy land inscribed
to my mother from a friend in the armed
forces *bill, jerusalem 1941*   *flowers and*
views of the holy land   it says inside   in three
languages   hebrew   english   french   each of twelve
oblongs of card has a sprig of pressed flowers glued
to its back   twelve hand tinted images of various
iconic scenes: deep and rich as illuminated dreams;
the flowers' colours have faded   the tissue interlaid
turned brown   but mostly the shapes of the tiny leaf
sprigs are firm and resolute; one flower has lost its
leaf and stalk but its red petals reveal a patient
heart   the vanished stalk has left a pale
imprint   it endures, this tenacious ghost –
as a three year old i visited bill's rose bay home
in a block of flats in balfour road   a name that
matters   like allenby street in the picture of old
tel aviv   underneath the main inscription he had
written, now in purple ink *more & more & still more –*
of all you wish yourself   i'm trying to keep this
poem simple just 'flowers from the holy land' like
an intact reverie   but this old gift of a book leans

unprotected never gathering dust on a poetry shelf
two down – i suddenly note – from 'selected
poems of darwish', born 1941, galilee
where did his 'carnations' grow ~

[The *carnations* image comes from a Mahmoud Darwish poem 'I Have Witnessed the Massacre']

stent

a golden morning   the harbour gleaming
all the way to manly margaret adores the
stillness in the air time to settle back with
'dracula'

as if on cue it starts the stentorian leaf
blower down below in the concrete car
park, noise spreads like an epidemic
through her ears – stoker's words are
swept away – she grabs the binoculars
hanging off the door the leaves are few
and tiny this blower of leaves wanders
east and west with his appliance – waving
the instrument around where there are no leaves
at all; margaret feels like grieving at this
extravagance: noise for noise's sake no relative
of art for art's sake on the proverbial family tree

margaret is about to pray to her favourite god/goddess
of silence when all goes quiet ah peace bright
wings she leaves abraham stoker's novel open at
page 92 'log of the *demeter*' and confirms no human
is now in the carpark; her ears begin to groan someone
upstairs is rehearsing 'danny boy' in full blown soprano
style again

amen

[with apologies to gerard manley hopkins]

shutters

a stockpile of crime
fiction to glide through
inside christmas   a cosyness
of birth death rebirth   this summery
staycation   guns forensics fists and
gods   warm blood thrums as you savour
one death then another another   sip cool
g&ts suck on tamarind tiger prawns
digest dark plums of best seller fear
mediated humid

downstairs along the greasy mile
bashings stabbings screeches and screams
cheap deals of powders and pellets mashed
evidence in the gutters dreary dull
unframed you reach for another novel
& douse your mouth with mango

watch tower   a reconnaissance

scene I

you slump in darkness gazing at
a screen   websites of a sleepless
night absorb the growing yawn   a
droopy eye glimpses a presence splayed
along the desktop tower an inch or two
away   a shape vigilant as silence:
a huntsman spider, yes – it has no
password   has it stolen yours

scene II

you creep into the kitchen for
a plastic bag to transfer this intruder
somewhere outside [you fear a trenchant
tenancy] before it slips or leaps away into
the torchless dark   no luck   it's moved
on ~ you google its behaviours, ways of
catching huntsmans   no, you don't want
to paralyse it with hairspray, handy hints!!

scene III

you fetch a quiet black broom and tiny
torch   the floorboards underneath the carpet
creak   ah there it is – up on the highest
bookshelf sprawling across the crime fiction   it
has bypassed rejected twenty thirty other shelves

kafka borges duras cortazar nin bernard edward
lear et al.......and settled right above 'the silence
of the lambs'   amused amazed you leave it there
and creep back into bed   your partner seriously
still asleep   you lie awake all thumping heart
what if the spider's moved into the bedroom
pausing on the picture rail above, about to drop
down on your faces   no no you're up again

scene IV

you rush slowmo into the bathroom
turn on the light   the furtive traveller's
now exploring toiletries – syrian soap
st luke's powder for prickly heat its
trademark icon of an upright cobra
with an arrow through its head   you
are determined   this spider will exit
through the window <u>now</u>   you coax it
round the ceiling tickling the walls with
soft broom hair like a swish of palm fronds
it almost drops down on dusty memorabilia:
minnie & mickey mouse toothbrushes rose petals
nesting in the olive oyl jug her surprised black
eyes   then sudden as a bird or a quick breath
it's out the window   stillness spreads like gel
of cool voltaren   no living creature has been
harmed in the writing of this poem except
perhaps the poet

confit

although we might have chewed on the same
page we never lived on the same continent
my new revised atlas confirms that   i am
not of the same stock cube as you   i filched
those cubes to add flavour to my misdemeanours;
you coveted my watermelon thongs although they
were the wrong accessories for your cassock your
whiskey profile made me lie so i could extract
myself more rapidly   i never left the hose
on or stole the prunes   i just needed something
to declare in that claustrophobic broth   your wry
desire left nothing to the imagination but a throb
of narcolepsy   how many strings of beads went
rusty while the candles gutted themselves   you had
too much cheek to turn things around   how many stuffed
holes in their shoes with the pages of your little black rule book
in the years of the credit squeeze   i spied you hurling a decomposed
fish down the aisle like a scarecrowed olympian   your motorcycle
slithering into the delta's bullrushes   its slick conspiracy

soak

cane soaking there in tubs and buckets lined up
on the long verandah ready for the creation
of twenty five breakfast trays   below, a morning of folk
dance practice always someone puking at the sight
of too-bright twirls of yellow skirts in a lowtide air

seven year old fingers weave the softened
cane into gifts for mother's day the insert of a
glossy strip of tangerine a decoration of the
heart, the glow of his sacrificial blood for ever
flickering through the class; that promise of the feather
duster's sting right behind the knees doled out to rectify
distraction, laughter, disobedience, in a gloomy
annexe its creaking chocolate wheel looming
down   that clack of sister mercy's waist-hitched
rosary beads   hell's tedious metronome

sleeve

the drive along the bay
from the library   furtive books
rose from your lap in waves
soldiers had just crossed the
hellespont from that desk perched
on the camouflaged sandhills
bus stop heads lounged outside
brilliantined milkbars   short sleeves
rolled tight and casual as testosterone's
gaze   'personality' jived around like a
candy bar in its own home movie   red
laminex crooned like a ouija board   these
were religious days

canary

today the harbour like lake placid no
new citizen whines in its suv stroller a
woman on a ferry waves with
some vigour to a boy in the frame
of a miniature window one of a million
on a mammoth cruise ship   'stupid
woman' i am urged to mutter   who
is she waving at so far away   the cruise
ship cancels the view of a shoreline's history
touro-imperialism on the 'catatonia'   let's
throw a lei towards the harbour's happy hour

i once bought a cane basket of some
sort or other i can't quite remember – a
one hour shore stop – the souvenir special,
at las palmas in the islas canarias   i'm on a greek
passenger ship lugging a stack of british migrants
and assorted others to the antipodes – a vessel
packed with holiday moments but just not for me
i couldn't keep all my eggs in one basket like a simple
farm girl or a blonde sunfrocked tourist eager to have
the best time of her life   i slouched and lurked
along the decks, close to regret and its shadows,
skeleton poems, the ache of long days; those acidic
stares and tut-tutty hisses from two calvinist matrons
at the five week assigned dining table, when my long
uncoiffed hair grazed their pristine bread rolls

a query or two

you might prefer a flat table
but that doesn't mean you
prefer a flat earth: query –
didn't that make the world go
round

is there a point to getting grumpy
if you're addressed as 'sir' by
a sushi seller or a supermarketeer –
better than being addressed as nothing
or no one   service is better for the sirs
of this world

do we need a term like
heteronormative   sounds
like a revamped incarnation
of milk   the fridges are bulging
already   is this the revenge of
the norms

you're feeling mega quizzical

as you proceed to leave
a mardi gras event at the
national art school, holding
a drink cup you're suddenly
circled by three security guards

with little to do amongst
a sparse crowd
                    it's only
kombucha you bluntly exclaim   there's
a stand off before you will get the green
light to depart   back you will go to the hospital
via green park   rainbow cup still in hand —
about to be dumped in the nearest green bin

query   *eerie*

lip

the reticent comic sprawls
across the numb linoleum considering
a loud tennis career   *pow-whoosh-slam*
but no one loves me anymore; delphic
teapots leak like hushed puppies   who
believes in loud prophecies these days
mountain tops prefer to sleep like blank
cassettes   would you want to wear high
heels into yodelic canyons   better to consult
a squad of kookaburras with zips on their
beaks –

[a riff on 'echo' from *on a clear day*]

the random couch

mercy

an hour glass hip hops
in the southern dunes late
for the late train   luggage
lost   somewhere between here
and returnity   fly with
the high risers, their feral surprises
ephemera of concrete dust flirts
with intuition   start from scratch
like a changeling novice   mosquitoes
end and begin   a bevvy of prophets
extract yourself from ayn rand's
toothbrush   self rescue on
the somnambulance express

lemon aid

a life not even hyphenated or
conjunctive   the jump cuts are
blunted or bloated   intent
suspended like a defused twelve fin
heater

in the salon of social opera
the gilt quietly peels off
the arches of gilbert and
george   best to sit low in
the high chair of comatoastie
mirrors and wait for a budget
shampoo or a letter unexpected
do we know who we really r

turret

this year
why a kilo of dragons
in lieu of a rapier
wit   better still leap
frog from the chapter
and you're in mitre 10
a discounted desk fan
red as a jousting cardinal
preens on its box   but
we're expecting some bang
for our buck   the barbecue
special is yesterday's frolique
the golden step ladder the
clairvoyant of choice   free
delivery   when you purchase a moat

scrub

fog in the throat hocked
household lyrics the
garage door collapsing
like a lung the rooms unravel
rows of bad knitting no one
sings for supper when the dunce
corner proliferates up
the walls = scouting for scraps
in the itchy bins tipped
across the verges' placid
shrubbery reinstall the skeletal
lighthouse some fine white
jokes to be launched through the night

entrée

is that you on the radio
mumbling through the fan's
dedication   my head awry
with b-p-p-vertigo why benign
why paroxysmal   all the
whirrings   it's hard to interpret
anything   though the birdsong
outside brings a thimble of respite –
always a song somewhere even if
it's kitsch   that season of the red
red robin that keeps on bob bob
bobbin' along x2 i need to keep still

now i'm thinking slowly, domingo
of donald trump and his significant dinner
at mar-a-lago [yes it rhymes with
'embargo'] with shinzo abe what is the
significance between the news of kim jong
un's big missile moment and their entrée
of iceberg lettuce gleaming with a dressing
of creamy blue cheese   a mind is a curious
thing where did lucy in the sky with diamonds
go –

crunch

fulfilling those dreams
with cornflakes wasn't as easy
as it smelt   faux crunch of
the necromancer   ankle
wrinkles don't disappear with
a spray and wipe can you
bear a curse of no_winged
sandals   the sun shines too
much   you're the busy old
foole hatless in the lethargic
plaza   the grounds shift
bitter beneath your eyes
such an indifferent barista
you grab at the walls of
next week's hallways   it
all seems so familiar

Acknowledgements

Australian Poetry Collaboration, *Australian Poetry Journal*, *Arc* (Canada), *Canberra Times*, *Cordite*, *Journal of Poetics Research*, *Mascara*, *Overland*, *Social Alternatives*, *Southerly*, *Western Humanities Review* (USA), *A Patch of Sun: Cafe Poets' Anthology 2016*, *Best Australian Poems 2014*, *2016–17* (Black Inc), *Contemporary Australian Feminist Poetry* (Hunter 2016), *'To End All Wars'* (Puncher & Wattmann 2018), *'Writing to the Wire'* (UWA 2016).

In the poem 'keyboard', *the duke of darlo-road* [or Darlinghurst Road] refers to a Kings Cross figure from the 1950s.

The Giramondo Publishing Company acknowledges the support of Western Sydney University in the implementation of its book publishing program.

This project has been assisted by the Commonwealth Government through the Australia Council, its arts funding and advisory body.